Empath Personal and Spiritual Healing

Harnessing Your Gift for the Highly Sensitive Person

Disclaimer

The author and publisher of this eBook have used their best efforts in preparing it. The author and publisher make no representation or warranties with respect to the accuracy, applicability, or completeness of the contents of this resource.

The information contained in this eBook is strictly for educational purposes. Therefore, if you wish to apply the ideas contained herein, you are taking full responsibility for your actions.

Trademarks mentioned in this book are property of their respective owners and may not be used without written permission. The fact that organizations, or websites are referred to in this work as examples does not mean that the author endorses the information, the company or website.

Readers should be aware that the information listed in this work may have changed or disappeared between when this book was written and when it is read.

Table of Contents

Chapter 1: Are you an Empath? 3

Chapter 2: The False Self 13

Chapter 3: The Phases of Development of an Empath 19

Chapter 5: Living in Society with Your Gift 30

Chapter 6: Reasons for Not Healing 33

Chapter 7: Empath Healing Techniques .. 37

Chapter 8: Repressed Sexuality 43

Chapter 9: Finding Your True Self 47

Chapter 10: Recharging 50

Conclusion 53

Introduction

If you are one of those hundreds of empaths who are desperately seeking answers to their questions about themselves and their situation, then you have come to the right place. The concepts and ideas you need to know about your empathic abilities will be explained to you by this book, piece by piece.

During the first few parts, this book will discuss the meaning, as well as the distinct traits of an empath. You will also be guided to your understanding about the concept of false self and how the society affects its development. There is also a breakdown of the phases or stages through which empaths undergo to develop themselves and become skilled empaths.

This book is also going to focus on discussing the core wound, the manifestations of having one, and how it is healed. It will also discuss the hindrances to healing it and of course, the techniques to mend it. You will also learn how to cope with the society and live in it as a free empath, with your sensitivity and abilities.

The latter part will tackle certain issues on being an empath particularly the sexual repression, and the challenge of finding one's true self. Lastly, once you have gained enough knowledge about yourself and your empathic abilities, the book will provide recharging methods that you may use occasionally, to maintain positivity as well as emotional and spiritual balance. So, if you want to start your journey to clarity and self-appreciation, proceed to chapter one!

Chapter 1: Are you an Empath?

Empaths, in the simplest terms, are sensitive individuals. However, there are so many things beyond this plain description that the world needs to understand. Things that hold the true meaning of being an empath. These are the vast gray scale that are often left blurred and ignored because the world is so used to simplifying things into either black or white. Being an empath is not a choice between black and white. It is not even a choice to begin with. You are either born an empath, or you are not.

Empaths feel people's emotions with their sensitivity consciously, or subconsciously. This means the feelings they get from other people's emotions are not necessarily under their own control. An empath can feel the emotion behind a certain person, without the need to hear that person speak. There are also instances where an empath can feel the true emotion behind a modified tone. So, it does not matter if the person speaks in a joyful tone. If he is sad, he will sound sad to an empath. If people hear voices, empaths feel them.

There are empaths who can easily read emotions through people's eyes. There are some who can sense feelings through smell. There are even empaths who tend to refrain from eating meat because they feel like they are tasting the animal's suffering. Overreaction? No. Feelings, for an empath, come in the form of sight, sound, taste, smell, and physical contact. The ability to sense things even in the absence of an actual intention to feel them is like a built-in enhancement to all their senses.

Empaths' abilities are not limited to emotions, by the way. They can also sense physical suffering and can even have tendencies to adopt such illness. Yes, it happens to empaths. Sometimes the physical pain, aches, and fatigue are a result of absorbing too much emotions from people. Empaths are also spiritually connected to human beings. Although often misunderstood, they often have the greatest, unending hope for humanity.

By knowing these things, you may now start identifying whether you are an empath or not.

But let me tell you one thing—the fact that you are reading this right now, chances are you are an empath. And to help you confirm that, here are the general characteristics that empaths naturally possess:

Ability to Easily Feel the Emotions of Other People

As an empath, you are more focused on your external surroundings and that gives you the ability to have a deeper understanding of your environment, particularly people. You don't need to hear people saying "I'm sad," to know that they are. The moment you see them, feel them, or hear them, you can already sense the emotions they are holding inside themselves. Emotions are always naturally transferred to or shared with you, with or without your conscious knowledge.

Carrying Others' Burden

In general, people can only truly understand someone's struggle if they, themselves, have experienced the same. Empaths do not usually require initial experience to understand the burden a certain person carries on his shoulders. Also, majority of people do not know the difference between knowing what other people feel and understanding what they are going through; but empaths do. And because of that, they often end up carrying others' burdens.

Sense of Truth
You know things well because you observe them. You know what's true and what's not. Although there is no solid scientific explanation to support this, it is almost only because this ability does not come from your physical senses, nor your guts, nor your intuition. It is a natural feeling that you get when you are listening to people.

Getting Others' Physical Symptoms
As once mentioned above, empaths are not just sensitive to people's emotions. Their sensitivity extends even to other people's physical pain and suffering. This does not only happen by mere physical touch or transfer of airborne virus, although this could be a factor. They also have tendencies to get sick or feel unwell once they feel the weariness the other person is feeling.

Overwhelmed by Public
Unless needed, you do not prefer staying in a public place. Public is a place where a number of varying energies from different people meet.

It is a huge pool of different emotions gathering all at once, and what's worse than uncontrollably getting somebody else's suffering is acquiring a lot of them from many people.

Do you possess most or all of these traits? If yes, it is safe to assume now that you are an empath. Do not worry, though as these are not the only things empaths have as their characteristics. There are several specific attributes that you may also relate to, and may help you further affirm your empathic trait.

You Feel Suffering Even on Screen
Do you sometimes turn off the TV when you see news about tragic events? Do you switch channels because of a mere commercial about violence? Or do you usually feel the desire to help the protagonist of a certain movie, just because he was being mistreated and bullied by the antagonist? If yes, it is most probably because empaths like you, do not need to be in the actual scenario to feel what is happening in there.

You Need Time to Be Alone
Solitude is your favorite escapade when things are getting rough and many people are getting unbearably emotional. Even when you don't

always grant yourself some time to be alone, you always tend to long for it. It is normal for empaths. Being alone is your opportunity to free yourself from any stress and gather energy to move and to face the world again.

You Are Deeply Connected to Nature

You enjoy being with other living things. You talk to dogs, cats, birds, and any other animals. Despite not getting response from them, you believe they can feel and understand you. You believe they are a part of your existence and you tend to get attached to them more deeply than other people do.

Your heart is always close to nature, as well. The fresh wind from the trees relaxes you just as much as the sound of ocean waves do. You feel free when you are on the mountains, or on the beach, or under trees. Nature feeds the spirits of empaths.

You Are Fond of Adventures

Your connection to nature is the bottom line of this trait. Either you love travelling or you enjoy the thought of it in case you haven't travelled yet. Nature gives you the freedom to breathe in the positive energies and breathe out the negativities. You love going to different places and feel as if your existence is a part of their history. You are a free spirit, just like any other empath.

You Get Bored Easily
Once you see things are getting less interesting, you get bored. You tend to make your life more exciting and more stimulating to keep yourself going. Distractions are your enemy. You start losing focus on doing a certain thing once you feel like working on it is unnecessary and won't give you anything. You tend to look for changes and modifications just so you could save yourself from totally losing interest on one thing.

You are Creative
Empaths have hidden talents, and some are lucky to have discovered theirs already. All of these talents link to the fact that empaths are naturally creative individuals. You prefer creating things out of basically anything. You have a deep passion for creation and a great sense of art, too. Painting, writing, drawing, or playing musical instruments are just some of the dominant talents empaths usually possess although there are still hundreds of talents that you, and all the other empaths can discover in yourselves.

You Love to Daydream
With your tendencies to get bored easily plus your creativity, you are consequentially prone to the habit of daydreaming. Whether you are at home or you are in class, or even when somebody is talking to you, if things get boring, you daydream. Being able to daydream just means your mind is healthy; but daydreaming all the time is something which is not anymore associated with being an empath.

You Always Seek for Knowledge
As an empath, you have an intense passion to seek answers for your questions. Doubts make you feel uneasy. Also, you never want your mind idled. You feed it with continuous knowledge about different things, mostly those which interest you. You are always curious about things that you do not know much about. You are always eager to learn new things.

You Hate Rules
This does not mean you are a rebel, though; that's a different thing. You don't like rules because you feel like you are being controlled. You never liked it when your freedom is being taken from you. Remember, empaths are free spirits.

You Always Look Out for the Outcasts
The bullied, the so-called nerd, the fat kid at school who never had a friend, you always see them from afar and feel the desire to be friends with them. You know that they are the talented people, the smart ones, or simply the people who also want to feel appreciated.

You Hate Egocentrics
This is not a surprise for somebody who has been spending his life caring about people and trying to help them all the time. Egocentrics are your total opposite and you never liked their tone. You do not tolerate selfishness as you think it is one of the primary reasons why the world is experiencing violence and hate instead of harmony and love.

You Appear Shy
You often do not feel the need to talk too much and that leads people to the misconception that you are shy. Some empaths are shy, most especially when they do not know how to handle their abilities. Some empaths, however, are used to engaging in conversation. Confidence is more or less a matter of experience and is not necessarily about whether you are an empath or not.

You Are an Excellent Listener

Since you are more concerned about your surroundings than yourself, you tend to be more welcoming to other people's confessions, sentiments, stories, and opinions. People love it when they confess to you. You listen sincerely to them. You give pieces of advice and sometimes, inspiring words to make them feel better. You listen because you want to understand people, and not because you just want to have something to hear about them.

Chapter 2: The False Self

If you could relate to all or most of the signs listed in the previous chapter, then I can guarantee that you are an empath. However, what I cannot guarantee, is your feeling or reaction toward it. Are you surprised? Are you sad? Or are you feeling indifferent? Or maybe happy?

If you are one of those few gifted empaths who are born with an indestructible optimism, that does not get broken despite absorbing an overwhelming amount of raw emotions, then most probably, you are happy about being an empath. If you are not, though, there is nothing to worry. I, together with a lot of empaths out there, have been there.

There may be moments in your life when you think you are better off without these excessively sensitive emotional senses. Or worse, you carry these thoughts every day. You are not the only one. I mean as an empath, who doesn't get worried about having a tendency to destroy his own day just because of the mere fact that he is sensitive? Being able to empathize with everyone's feelings is just, sometimes, too much to handle. Plus, you are often misunderstood for it. Sadly, other people can't seem to find time to understand empaths like us. So, they judge us, bully us, or ignore our feelings, instead. And this often leads to an empath, creating an entity whom everyone likes, but nobody truly knows about—the false self.

The Idea of False Self
A handsome, dashing guy with a perfect pleasing personality who walks along the corridor feeling cool and confident, while the girls in his school are dying just to get his number. With his spotless academic record of straight As, and his pro baseball and basketball skills, he inspires almost anybody. There is only one problem about him, though—he's not real.

But I once wanted to be him. I created him because I loved the idea of being able to stand out, the feeling of superiority and invulnerability, the comfort of happiness because you know people are not randomly judging you on a daily basis. I tried to be him but unfortunately, I could never be him. He was my false self... Or maybe yours too.

According to the American physician and psychotherapist, Alexander Lowen, your false self is the version of yourself that you present to the world. It is what rests on the surface and is the opposite of what is inside. What is inside is your true self, which you hide as you deem it weak and unwanted.

The idea was originated and introduced by the psychoanalyst, Donald Winnicott. "Defensive facade" was Winnicott's perception to the false self and he said that people who project false selves could end up feeling empty, and lifeless inside.

What Triggers the Creation of False Self?

1. **Society** - this is where empaths meet other people. The kindness of empaths is often mistaken as weakness and susceptibility. Other people tend to judge, and belittle them. Some people perceive empaths to be annoyingly thoughtful and reserved. They want to make people like empaths level themselves down to what is "normal." Being outnumbered, most of the

empaths choose to just change themselves instead of trying to prove their uniqueness. Thus, they try to blend in and worse, lose their true selves in the process.

2. **Standards** - the norms of the society, though not always right, always dominate the odds. The society has been caging its people with its exacting standards ever since the beginning of time. Empaths find it hard to cope with a society that is primarily concerned with the loud, dominant, and open personalities. Since these characteristics are what comprise the majority of society, they are often considered as the "normal" traits.

There are also cases where empaths start to develop their fake selves as early as childhood. It can start with the standards of their own family, in their own home. Parenting plays a vital role in the development of an empathic child's perception of what he will be in the future. If parents keep on forcing their child to perform well in school, or to be good at a certain talent or subject; chances are the child will grow believing that he must be someone whom his parents want him to be.

There is nothing wrong with guiding a child to be great at things that will help him in the future, but parents should not forget that, what the child has is his own life, and not an extension of theirs.

3. **Self-doubt** - Just because you do not physically participate much in the society, or you grew up in a liberal family, does not mean you are safe from suppression. The creation of false self is ultimately dependent upon you, yourself. Since you are an empath, it is likely that you regard your decisions in life based on how you think others may feel about them.

Your own idea about your self is of paramount importance when it comes to your decisions in life. If you are confident enough, you are not easily influenced by the energies that subconsciously enter you. On the other hand, if you are in doubt of your own capabilities, you are more likely to develop a different persona to appear perfect and invulnerable <u>at the cost of your true self</u>.

As an empath, your potential capability of creating another person in you serves either as a defense mechanism, against the society and its standards; or as a permanent escape, to be able to completely erase the idea of your seemingly weak, true self.

It is vital that as early as this point, you are already aware whether you are pretending to be someone else or not. Let me ask you, "are you, you?" Before we proceed to the next chapter, answer the question as honest as possible. Trust me, the last person you would want to lie to—is yourself.

Chapter 3: The Phases of Development of an Empath

Before understanding the stages, it is important to know that your false self is not the one who is going to undergo development; but your true self. You are an empath and you do not have to deny that, at least not here. But if you are still trying to get hold of your projected persona, it might be because you are still in the burdened phase. Don't panic though. The burdened phase is not your one and only destination as an empath. It is just among one of the empath's phases of development. There are actually seven of them and majority of the empaths haven't reached the seventh phase yet.

On the other hand, those who have reached the last stage are considered to be skilled empaths. Yes, they are still empaths. There is no way to lose it even when you reach the fifth, sixth, or seventh phase. Remember, the main problem of an empath is his uncontrolled ability to absorb an excessive amount of energy from his external environment. Thus, the key is to control it, and not to remove it. And If you want to know how and when you can gain such control, you need to be aware first of the seven phases of development to become a skilled empath.

According to Caroline van Kimmenade, a writer and a coach to highly sensitive people, there are seven phases toward becoming a developed or a skilled empath. These phases cover the stages from an empath's confused beginnings, which is the first phase, to an empath's confident and assertive stage, which is the seventh or last phase.

However, Kimmenade stated that the following phases are not strict instructions and are not supposed to narrow down your choices in life. An empath may jump from the second phase straight to the fifth phase if he happens to develop things fast. There is no hard and fast rule here. This is merely a list to serve as your guide to know under which phase of development your current situation falls.

The Burdened Phase
Under this are the episodes in your life where you feel like you are doomed with all the

emotions wrapping around you. You keep on uncontrollably receiving other people's burdens, to the extent where you cannot anymore identify which among these problems are yours and which are not. You keep on exhausting yourself because you feel like you are obliged to help all those who are in need.

As a defense, you try to appear strong and tough by any means without knowing you are unconsciously hurting yourself. You try to blend in. You try to adopt the norms. You feel like if you get to be normal like other people, things will be fine. This is generally the phase where false selves are created. (Sounds familiar!)

The Basic Self-care Phase

This is the phase where you start analyzing the internal energy that is coming from you. You are trying to focus on understanding more of your personal struggles instead of others'. You have taken some steps to take care of yourself and your own feelings. You try to isolate yourself sometimes. You try to rest when you get tired and you try to give yourself a break from stress.

This phase can be the result of you, getting tired of your own sensitivity. I hope, though, that you won't have to come to a point where you'll find yourself lost and weary before you can realize that you have to take care of yourself. Some empaths have immediately proceeded in this phase the moment they noticed that their sensitivity is getting out of hand.

The Energy Research Phase
If you are on this phase, you may have leveled up the measures you are taking to improve yourself. You are now utilizing different methods to help you gather more positive energy. You try to meditate or practice yoga. You use visualizations and music relaxation to somehow attain peace of mind.

The Empath Training Phase
You know you are still far from being a fully skilled empath but it does not bother you anymore. At this stage, you have learned to do things at your own pace. You are starting to notice improvements little by little. You can now join seminars, programs, and talks about empathy without being ashamed of yourself. Improving yourself is now more important than caring about what others may feel about you.

The Gaining Control Phase

You can now apply all the skills you have learned in the process to help you cope with the society. You can now live your own life without being so affected by everyone else's pain. You are starting to see your empathic ability as a gift rather than a curse. Although you still cannot fully control your ability, you know you have improved in terms of using it. Also, you can now somehow handle the forces that are entering you.

The Increasing Clarity Phase

You now have reprogrammed your subconscious through the help of the tools and methods you applied before. You are no longer under the control of your own emotions. Instead, you are now the one who controls them. You may pick energies from your external environment but you are able to lessen and control their impact to you.

The public does not scare you anymore. You don't get overwhelmed by an awful amount of forces around you. You are able to get along with people without having to contain all their pain and emotions. You don't get worried about how their energies can affect you anymore. You are now more into understanding how your energy can impact them in a positive way.

The Conscious Empath Phase
Your ability to feel others is now under your conscious control. You now have a deep understanding of yourself as an empath. Also, you are not afraid to feel the emotions of other people anymore. In fact, you are now interested in getting to know how others feel to help them cope with their own lives. You don't carry the burden of feeling like you are responsible for everything that is happening on the people around you.

You are now a skilled empath. A free spirit who can live his life confidently without having to forcibly change his image to be accepted. You understand that not everyone is going to accept you and that's completely fine with you. You may not be able to choose the energy you may come across, but it is certainly up to you whether you are going to let it enter you or not.

Think of it as having an invisible force field around you. You can still see things in clarity but you are now protected from all the energies around. Your consciousness has the switch to open and close the barrier whenever it wants. It can also control how wide you want the opening to be. It's an exceptional skill that all the empaths must acquire. Although it is not that easy to learn, I can definitely tell that it is worth all the struggles.

Chapter 4: The Core Wound

Going back to the first phase of development, the creation of false self is not the only thing that happens during such stage. The burdened phase is also the period where we accumulate the damages being brought by our troubles, shortcomings, and mistakes. It is when we become highly sensitive that our core becomes penetrable. As a result, we develop an internal wound that sometimes, not even time can heal—the core wound.

The core wound is the deepest, non-physical wound that we carry in ourselves throughout the majority of our lives. It is like an open wound except that it lies within our souls, and it does not bleed though it pains us heavily. It's the worst kind of damage as it can hurt us physically, emotionally, spiritually, and mentally. It weakens our grip on life. And what makes it the worst is that it could take a lifetime to heal.

The core wound can be developed as early as childhood. People who have experienced suppression, abuse, or rejection when they were young would carry such experiences until the latter part of their lives. The way we handle mistakes, insecurities, judgments, and unhealthy relationships unconsciously worsens the wound. The thing is, a lot of people are not aware that their core wounds are getting worse and worse each day. And if you are one of these people, let me help you identify the signs of having a grievous core wound.

Manifestations of Having a Severely Damaged Inner Core

You're Too Hard on Yourself
Every time you make mistakes, you blame yourself. Every time you don't achieve the things that you want, you feel like you are useless. You keep on telling yourself, "I don't count," "I'm pathetic," or "Who am I anyway?"

You Feel Incomplete
You easily get insecure. You try hard to be like other people. You are always looking for somebody to complete you as if you are not whole in the first place. And as a result, you end up getting into premature and unhealthy

relationships that don't last; and worse, make you feel like you are not worth any person's love, or you are hated, or you can never be accepted.

You Consider Yourself an Outcast
Your poor appreciation of yourself leads to you, thinking that you do not belong to any circle. You don't try socializing that much because you are afraid that your traits won't pass the society's standards of "normality." You think people do not want you as their friend when in fact it was actually just you, who made up such thought.

Your False Self is Your Exact Opposite
Some people create false selves that appear to be a better version of themselves. Some focus on modifying only certain aspects of their personality that they think are unacceptable. But you? You create a whole new different person out of your utmost desire to feel invulnerable. You tend to change everything as you think you are not supposed to be who you are. You cover your kindness with a violent personality. You protect your ego by denying your mistakes. You replace love with hatred. You reject people, compete with them, or try to control them, all because you do not want to feel weak.

Healing the Core Wound

Healing the core wound is not as easy as cleaning a cut and letting it dry up with your skin's automatic regeneration. Unfortunately, your soul does not have that "automatic regeneration" ability. You, yourself should work your way to your own soul's healing. Your physical capacity and mental focus are important for your recovery but you should concentrate more on your <u>emotional and spiritual states,</u> as these are the ones that affect your sensitivity.

Your emotional state may be enhanced by emotion-enhancement programs, relaxation music, physical trainings, solitude, and anti-anxiety exercises. Your spiritual state, on the other hand, may be enhanced through meditation, water therapy, healing tools like flower essences, crystals, and oils. These will be further elaborated in chapter 7. The important thing for now, is that you know that an empath's core wound can be healed despite his hypersensitivity to external energies.

Chapter 5: Living in Society with Your Gift

The question is, how do empaths like us, live in a society largely consists of extroverted, strong, and loud personalities?

Let's start with an empath's sensitivity. Other people are less affected to what is happening to their surroundings unless they see its significance to their personal lives. Empaths, on the other hand, tend to feel involved in almost everything that happens. We, empaths, tend to care more about this world and as a result, we often <u>lose time for ourselves</u> and spend much of it helping, or thinking about the society. That is what's normal to us and it doesn't have to be changed. Continue helping. You may not receive any return from it but I'm sure, the galaxies are thanking you from afar.

Our listening skill is what this society also needs so try to offer more of it and don't be ashamed of it. A lot of people out there need to vent their emotions, release their feelings, or confess their deepest secrets but unfortunately, everybody seems to be so busy with their personal issues. Nobody seems to be interested in listening as people tend to consider their own lives as the only interesting thing to discuss about. In a world full of people who keep on talking about themselves, empaths are the ones who are always ready to listen.

We can feel other people's core wound because we are spirituality sensitive as well. Regardless how people try to hide it or deny it from us, we can feel the pain they are holding in themselves. You don't have to force other people to open up. Just let them know that people like you, who understand the burden they are carrying, exist. You should not feel guilty about not being able to help them to the fullest because trust me, the fact that they know they have somebody to share their problems to whenever they are ready, is a huge relief to them.

It is completely ironic how we, empaths spend our lives trying to understand and help other people yet most of us can't even understand ourselves. It just means that you are greater than what you think you are. Just imagine how much more help you can offer to people once you fully understand yourself.

 Of course, understanding yourself is not as easy as feeling every energy around you. There are a lot of things that you need to let go of first before you can truly accept yourself and your abilities, such as your hate toward your own personality and your fear of being not enough for other people. Also, there are things in yourself that you need to mend such as your misconceptions about your empathic ability, the way you handle situations, and most importantly, your own core wound.

Chapter 6: Reasons for Not Healing

Empaths often overlook the significance of their personal choices and actions in life. They even mistake some of their customs as effective to help them heal their core wounds yet the truth is, they are not. So, instead of having their inner wound healed, it just gets worse and worse each day. It would take a lifetime to discuss all the reasons that are possibly hindering the healing of an empath's core wound. So, I've come up with a list to present to you some of these reasons that are particularly important, as they are the ones that empaths normally do every day.

Living the People-pleaser Personality
You try so hard to be accepted when acceptance is not something you force in the first place. When people ask you to change, you'll more or less change yourself unhesitatingly. <u>You project your false self in front of other people because you think it suits the society.</u> You keep on trying to change what's on the outside without realizing that you are already hurting inside.

33

Letting Someone's Behavior Destroy You
With your desire to please people, you try to endure everyone's behavior. You let them hurt you, bully you, make fun of you because you think that is how you make friends with people. You think that getting used to their destructive behavior will eventually lessen your sensitivity and make you stronger but unfortunately, it won't.

Doing Others' Workload
You take "helpfulness" to the next level. You try to do others' tasks, works, or assignments because you think it will increase your chance of being accepted. You overwork, stress yourself out, and exhaust yourself just to find out that you are being treated as a pet and not as a friend.

Scapegoating Yourself
You keep on taking the blame on behalf of your friends, your family, or other people. Your guilt toward things makes you feel like you are responsible for everything and that it is just right to put the blame on you. You think catching the damage for others would help them cope with the situation and would help your relationship with them get stronger.

Tolerating Abuse
You keep on giving other people chances regardless of how much they wasted your time and your feelings. You often disregard the bad things that people did to you. You are <u>afraid of losing them</u> because you think your life will be empty once they leave. So, you keep on chasing after them at the cost of your own self-worth. Your core wound is getting worse and worse but you can't feel it because your <u>martyrdom</u> is making you numb.

Depending on Drugs
You are so damaged that you think drugs are your safest escape. You take endorphins, antidepressants, anxiolytics or anti-anxiety drugs as they are the easiest way to drop down your sensitivity level. Yes, these drugs can temporarily provide relief and comfort but they are not the only solution available. At the end of the day, none of them are making things better.

Codependency
You rely so much on other people, particularly to your partner. You think things are always better when you have a companion around you. It may be true to some extent though; but depending your life, your actions, and your

decisions solely on other people can ruin you. You are barely living your own life and you are losing your self-worth, piece by piece.

Chapter 7: Empath Healing Techniques

Empath healing can be done in two ways: prevention of further infliction and taking measures to heal yourself. The first way is to let time alone heal it. You need to, however, protect the core wound from getting worse by preventing the hindrances—listed in the previous chapter—that may hurt your chances of getting spiritually healed. The second way on the other hand, is done by healing the wound by yourself, using the following tools and practices:

Meditation
Meditation is the key to peace of mind and peace of mind is one of the keys to your healing. Meditation helps you clear all the chaotic and toxic thoughts that are poisoning your mental energy. It aligns the thoughts in your mind that are in complete disarray, as these are the reason you cannot come up with proper decisions in life.

Meditation comes in many types like the "mindfulness" meditation, originating from the Buddhist tradition, which is done by closing your eyes while sitting on crossed legs, with your back straight. The relaxation comes from breathing in and out, and is meant to release depression. You can also try the visualization method of meditation that is a more modern technique. It is a guided meditation done by watching a sequence of scenes or images, along with a voice guiding you throughout the process. There are actually a lot of methods to perform meditation. You just need to choose which among them suits your needs.

Laughter
You release all the negative vibrations inside you when you laugh. Laughter serves as your personal vibe converter because it can transform negative energies inside you into positive ones. Laughing is the simplest method of healing yourself and the best thing about it is that, it does not cost anything. Brighten up your life by laughing every day as it accelerates your healing process.

Discovering Your Outlets
You have learned in the previous chapters that empaths are born with creativity. The good

news is, you can actually use yours to help yourself heal. Discover your hidden talents or in case you have already discovered them, nourish them. You may choose to paint, draw, write, sing, dance, compose, cook, or anything that could distract you, whenever you feel like you are starting to get covered by an unwelcoming atmosphere of varied energies. Use your talents to serve as your outlets for unreleased emotions like joy, gloom, hatred, or love. What's better than having an instant outlet to vent your feelings is the fact that you can also improve your talents through it.

Nature

An empath's spiritual energy is naturally linked to nature. This is the reason why some empaths possess the talent of geomancy in their subconscious. Provide yourself at least a weekly dose of nature interaction. Stay under a tree, swim in the fresh waters, or go into nature adventures. Your sensitivity allows you to absorb more of the positivity of nature so avail yourself of this healing method if you need a deeper contact to serenity.

Water

Dehydration does not only happen when you literally lack water in your body. It also happens to your soul. Fortunately, water doesn't just relieve physical dehydration but also the body's spiritual thirst. Water is your ultimate ally. It has a lot more function and importance to you than you think.

According to Dr. Masaru Emoto, a Japanese researcher, author and the photographer behind the volume "Messages from Water," emotional vibrations and emotional energies could change the water's physical structure. The conclusion was based on Doctor Emoto's water crystal experiment. Different water from different sources like river, lake, and water facilities, were frozen into crystals. The structures of crystals were observed to be different from each other. Frozen crystals from water that came from sources that are near industrialized areas didn't show beautiful crystals. On the other hand, crystals from fresh, virgin lakes and rivers developed beautiful crystal formations.

The experiment was further developed when Doctor Emoto started experimenting the effects of different actions to water as they are being frozen. Doctor Emoto tried playing music to water, showing letters and pictures to water, and praying to water. It was then found out that beautiful crystals are formed after offering prayer, giving good words, and playing good music to water while opposite actions resulted into disfigured crystals.

Based on Doctor Emoto's experiment, water can be considered as an element that absorbs energies that come from its environment. Let the water release the negative energy in you through cleansing and urination. And let clarity and positivity flow into your spirit through rehydration and refreshment.

Sea Salt

Seawater has a potent wound-healing factor. Sea salt, which is basically the solidified version of sea water and its minerals—can actually be an empath's healer. Since it is easily transferred into the bloodstream, it immediately helps clear out unwanted energy and dissolves negativity from your body.

Among the thousands of choices, the best one for an empath is the Himalayan sea salt. If the usual table salt has only four trace minerals and elements, the Himalayan sea salt contains 84 of them. You can pair your water intake with this salt to accelerate healing. Just dissolve a small amount on your tongue before drinking a glass of water.

Oils

Essential oils particularly target the skin, as well as the olfactory senses, to relax and balance emotional energy within your body. You can also inhale the vapors from essential oils. The limbic system is the part of the brain that is known to have a significant impact on one's emotions. Also, the oil's therapeutic benefits can be easily absorbed by the skin once the oil is applied on it. Oils are more into balancing the hormones and uplifting the spirit with its smooth texture and relaxing fragrance.

Lavender oil is the most versatile oil for an empath; it has tonic effects, and relaxing aroma. Plus, it has antibacterial and antiseptic agents. Basil and jasmine oils are perfect mood enhancers. Geranium and chamomile oils, on the other hand, are best for relaxing your mind state. Don't hesitate using oils as there will always be at least one that can address your current needs.

Chapter 8: Repressed Sexuality

Among the aspects of an empath's life, his sexuality receives the least attention. Why? Come to think of it. The murder or bombing scenes in a tv show are seemingly normal to watch with friends or family but when the sex scene comes, everything just gets awkward. That exact moment, already exhibits how discouraged the subject sexuality is in our society.

Sex is a normal function of humans; or at least it was before society and religion decided that it's not. Since society and religion both hold enough power to influence the majority, expressing sexuality has been considered unethical and immoral. This caused sexual repression to take place.

Being an empath entails an extra challenge to control sexual urges and desires. Sexual energies can bother us just as much as emotional energies do. The hardest part of dealing with them is making the decision to whether release them or keep them; but my advice? Release them.

Repressed Sexuality Can Change Your Energy

One of the reasons why I gave that advice is that sexual energy can possibly affect the flow of energy in your body. Yep, we are also prone to unwarranted changes in our own energy, as if not being able to control the energies that enter us is not hard enough. Empaths need to maintain balance among different energies that flow in their body including sexual energy. So, any excess sexual energy can cause imbalance which can eventually lead to mood changes, distractions, or intensified desires for sexual intercourse.

Sexual Energy Can Control Your Whole System

Sexual energy is usually stronger than most of the energies in your body. If you do not let go of it, it can control your thoughts, your actions, or your whole system. You may have experienced feeling a random orgasm in the middle of a supposedly serious moment like studying or working. So, instead of being productive, you spent the whole night distracted while trying to resist the urge.

Aside from random distractions, you may also experience chronic tension due to carrying too much energy within your lower belly.

Unfortunately, such accumulated energy is not released during orgasm. You may also acquire insomnia when your sexual energy is not properly channeled. These are just some of the many instances that may happen when sexual energies, in the form of sexual urges, are repressed.

Sexual Energy Might Burst Out

Have you ever thought how rapists could do such horrible things to people? It's possibly due to them, being sexually repressed that they couldn't anymore control the accumulated sexual urge. As an empath, you are supposed to release sexual energy from your body but instead, you tend to bury it in the deepest part of your soul. Hiding it might seem fine at first, until it bursts out of you in the ugliest way possible.

Since you are already aware of the probable effects of sexual repression, you now might be curious about how to release sexual energy. Considering our traits as empaths, we generally have two realistic methods of releasing sexual energy. You either feed it or transmute it into another subject.

Feeding your sexual desire does not necessarily mean sex although it is one of your options under this method. If you are going to have sex, make sure that you have trained your mental and emotional state beforehand. If you haven't done them yet, try the measures provided in chapter 7 to channel your energy into boosting your self-esteem. Remember, you need to be confident, assertive, and calm during sex otherwise things will be ruined. I strongly recommend, however, that you should only have sex with your partner. Loyalty is intimacy. It makes you feel more comfortable and connected with your partner. Aside from sex, you may also opt to watch pornographic material, masturbate, or read books about sex and relationships.

The second choice you have is transmutation. You may harness the sexual energy you have and transform it into a creative output. Instead of forcing yourself into sex despite not being ready, it would be safer and more beneficial if you use such energy to write a book about intimacy or paint an abstract with intense and warm colors. You can also try nude painting or photography. As I have mentioned earlier, sexual energy is a strong energy. Use it wisely.

Chapter 9: Finding Your True Self

"The truth will set you free."
Yes, it's a famous saying that will never get old, not until every empath on Earth finds his true self. Sadly, many empaths out there are still trapped in their own cages. Cages built with self-doubt and denial. If you happen to be one of those empaths, then it's about time to reconsider your life and start your journey toward freedom. And to guide you with that, below are the steps that will serve as your guide on your way to finding your true self.

Accept the Fact That You Are Lost
You don't find something that isn't lost. Therefore, unless you accept the truth that your true self is lost, you will never have the desire to find it. Set aside your pride and ego and focus more into accepting the idea of your loss. The sooner you accept it, the sooner you'll be able to start moving. In this journey, your point of view is everything so it is best to begin your adventure with a solid mindset.

Know What Your Heart and Mind Desire
What are the things that you live for? Always take note of the things that make you happy regardless how petty you think they are. They are usually the clues or hints that will guide you to the bigger picture—your passion. <u>Your passion is where your mind and heart meet.</u> Once you know what makes you happy, clarity and sense of purpose will follow. In short, your passion will be the one to set your direction.

Embrace Your Flaws
You have the mindset and the direction but the problem is, something's stopping you from moving forward. It is more likely your fear of the fact that you might just end up knowing your flawed and faulty self. It may actually be true if you want to see it that way; but you can also look at it as your opportunity to discover more of your strengths and abilities. You are just like any other human being who has both strengths and flaws. <u>Being aware of your weaknesses helps you know your limits and boundaries. That way, you'll know when to push yourself and when to stop.</u>

Letting Go of the Past and People in It.
The forces in your past will always have a strong hold on you and trust me, you do not

want to let it stay that way. Reminiscing about the good old days is fun. Remembering your past mistakes just brings guilt and regret. Regardless of how joyous or gloomy your experiences were, the past will never be the right place for you to dwell on.

It is also important to release all your hate, grief, insecurity, and love for the people who are already gone. Containing an overwhelming amount of unreleased emotional energies may just lead to emotional and spiritual imbalance. Learn to let go of them. Not everyone is going to stay. Try to let go of their memories, little by little, and start taking your own path with or without them. And remember, when you start walking, there is no turning back so keep moving.

Chapter 10: Recharging

Being an empath does not end the moment you finally found yourself. In fact, a more exciting life is just about to start right there. Once you fully embrace yourself, things will start falling into place. Only then will you realize that what you have in you is a gift. And you will be able to use that gift properly at your own will.

However, just because you can control your ability doesn't mean you are immune to exhaustion and meltdown. Always keep in your mind that you are an empath and you are meant to respond sensitively to energies around you. Because of that, you will be needing strategies to maintain balance whenever you run into draining situations. Even the skilled and strongest empaths out there know that they need to recharge themselves every once in a while. So, adopt their winning mindset and keep these recharging strategies in your mind to make yourself ready for any moments in life, even for the exhausting ones.

Take Micro Breaks

Micro breaks are healthy pauses that usually last 30 seconds to five minutes. As an empath, you battle not only with physically demanding tasks everyday but also with emotional energies that try to enter you. Because of that, you tend to receive more pressure than others. Use these micro breaks to temporarily distract you from work pressure and stress. They can also help you retain focus by relaxing your mind for a while and taking away unnecessary thoughts from it. These short breaks can make a huge difference when it comes to your health and productivity. Empaths who work for straight hours and push themselves beyond limits often end up destroying their health instead of being productive, while empaths who use micro breaks, though slower, usually maintain a steady working pace and a healthy flow of energy in their body.

Focus Your Energy on Your Importance

Keep your energies focused on your importance as it will not only establish a positive mindset, but will also protect you from unwanted forces that may negatively influence your actions and decisions. Through this, you will also learn how to appreciate yourself more. Your self-worth and your self-esteem are important to maintain a balanced flow of energy within you. Always keep the flow of your energy smooth and relaxed so you can control it more easily and appropriately, even when you are bombarded with a lot of negative forces from your external environment.

Conclusion

Being an empath is both a gift and a challenge. You possess a gift of having unique traits and abilities including the ability to easily feel other people's emotions, sense of truth, love for adventure, desire to be alone sometimes, deeper connection to nature, and other innate characteristics that make you feel more connected to the world.

Challenges, on the other hand, come in the form of trials like the challenge to find your true self behind the projection of your false self, healing your deepest core wound amid life struggles, and trying to overcome sexual repression that is brought by society. Every day, you battle difficulties that hinder your healing. You also undergo different phases to improve yourself as a person and as an empath.

Fortunately, there are several measures to help you cope with your empathic ability and at the same time, with the world. You can use healing techniques such as practicing meditation, releasing your emotions through your creativity, bonding with nature, and using oil, sea salt, and water to balance your energy, achieve peace of mind, and vitalize your soul. Furthermore, you can also try to regain positivity by recharging every once in a while; and that is done by taking micro breaks and by focusing more on self-appreciation.

Use all the learning you have gained from this book to understand and improve yourself. That way, you can understand and help other people as well. Empaths play a vital role in society. Harness your empathic ability to maximize your potentials. You can have the power to improve the vibrations in the atmosphere, turn the negative aura into positivity, and uplift other people, all of which can only be attained once you believe in your abilities. So, know your potentials, focus on your worth, recharge when needed, and most importantly, keep moving forward. And eventually, you will find yourself standing right in front of your own success.

Made in the USA
Lexington, KY
21 September 2017